Country Flat Carving with Tom Wolfe

Text by Douglas Congdon-Martin

1469 Morstein Road, West Chester, Pennsylvania 19380

Printed in the United States of America.
ISBN: 0-88740-278-X

Published by Schiffer Publishing, Ltd.
1469 Morstein Road
West Chester, Pennsylvania 19380
Please write for a free catalog.
This book may be purchased from the publisher.
Please include $2.00 postage.
Try your bookstore first.

Contents

Introduction

What we are calling country flatcarving has a long and glorious history. It is seen throughout the ancient world in one form or another, where it is called bas-relief. This kind of carving is done on a flat surface. The image is made to project outward by removing the background. Whether in the Great Pyramid or the sign down at the country store, the idea is the same.

Tom Wolfe has been carving signs and other flatcarvings for many years, bringing to them the same creativity and skill he brings to his three dimensional work. Sometimes practical, sometimes whimsical, and sometimes a little bit of both, this country flatcarving is loved by everyone.

Country Flatcarving shares some of Tom's patterns and techniques. The three projects include a potholder holder (practical), the man in the moon (whimsical) and a welcome sign (a little of both). You will find step-by-step instructions, all illustrated in full-color, and will be able to design and carve your own patterns when you are finished.

Tom Wolfe is an internationally known wood-carver. His studio is at Mystery Hill in Blowing Rock, North Carolina. He sells original work there as well as reproductions of his most popular carvings. Nancy Wolfe, Tom's wife, is a partner in this venture and they also join their talents to create country dolls.

Tom shows his work at many craft events around the nation and in Europe. His reproductions are finding an ever broadening market around the country.

In addition to *Country Flatcarving* Tom has shared his technique in several other books. Previously Schiffer Publishing has published *Country Carving, Pig Pickin'*, and *Country Dollmaking* (done with Nancy). Along with *Country Flatcarving* Tom is publishing two other books: *Santa and His Friends: Carving with Tom Wolfe*, and *Bears and Bunnies: Animal Carving*. All these books are available at your carving supply house, local book store or by writing to the publisher.

The Patterns

On the following pages you will find the patterns for the projects in the book, with a cow for good measure. Begin by tracing the patterns onto poster-board stock. You can copy the patterns by laying a piece of onion skin paper over them and tracing the lines. Then place a piece of carbon paper (carbon side down) on the cardboard. Put the onion skin tracing over that and go over the lines again with a pencil or ball point pen. With he proper pressure you should transfer the patterns to the posterboard which you can then cut out. Cut the pattern out of the posterboard and you are ready to go!

8

Carving the Potholder Holder

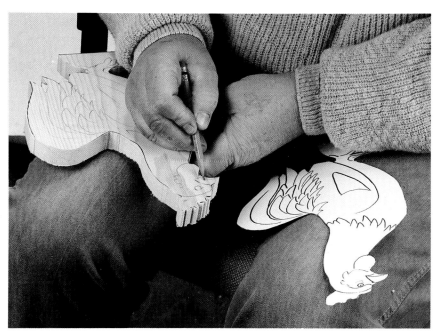

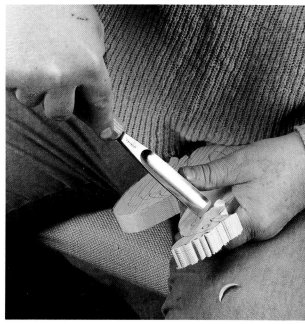

Draw the pattern on a piece of clear 1″ x 11″ white pine and cut it out with a band saw. People usually prefer to use a good sturdy table to do this carving and it is probably safer. After years of experience (and for the ease of photographing this project) I prefer to use my lap as a tool bench. This choice has cost me more than one pair of paints and a little blood.

For some curving areas you will use a gouge for the stop...

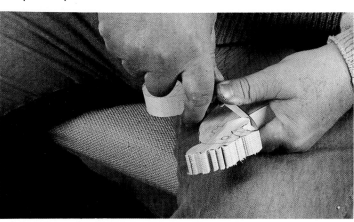

Start by making stops around the wattle with the knife.

and continue to use it to cut into the stop.

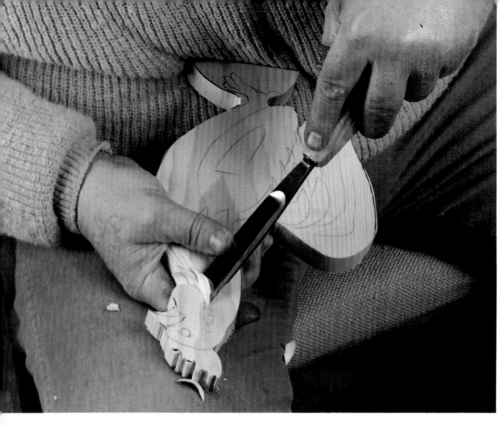

Another view of the gouge in use.

Use a smaller gouge to put stops around the upper part of the comb...

Clean up the cuts.

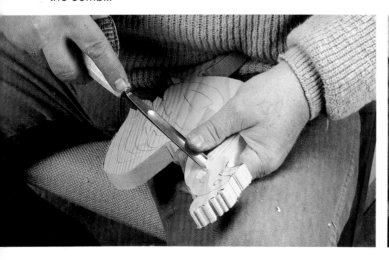

and cut back into it.

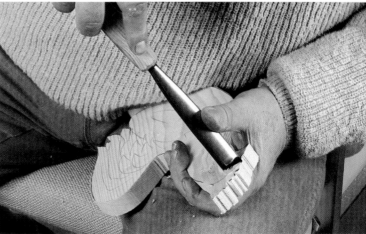

Cut a stop below the comb with the gouge.

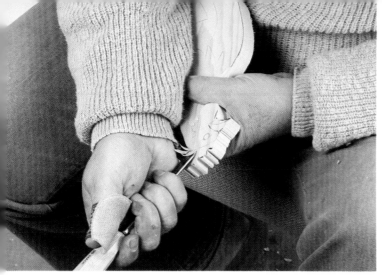

Cut back to it from the top of the head.

Continue working it down into a point.

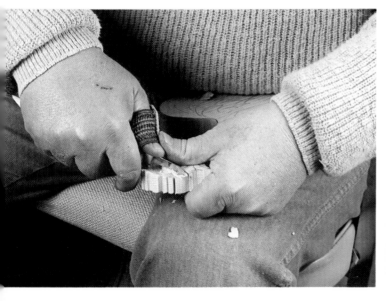

Deepen the comb cut using the gouge and the knife.

Also trim from the bottom of the beak.

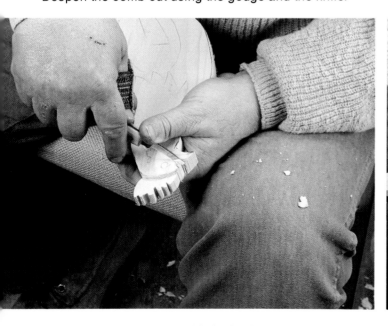

Shape the top of the bill with the knife.

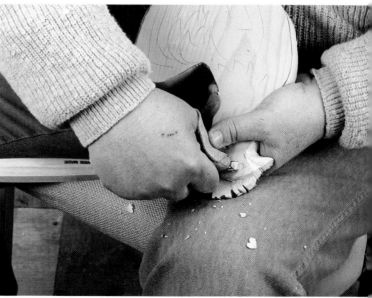

Gouge out the eye socket.

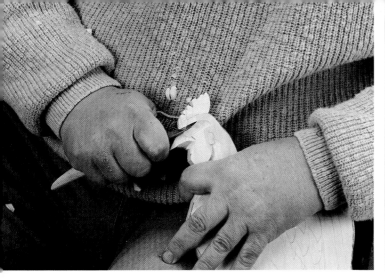

Then round off the forehead.

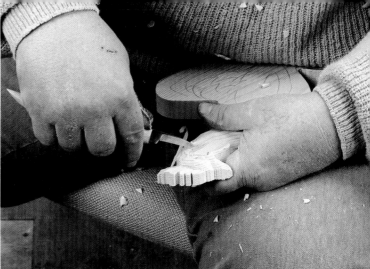

Trim back to the stops from the back of the head.

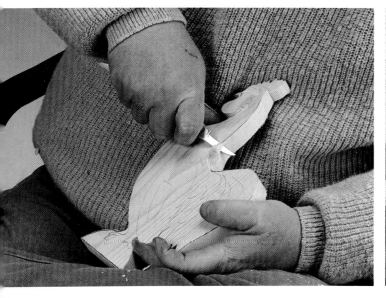

Round the back of the neck.

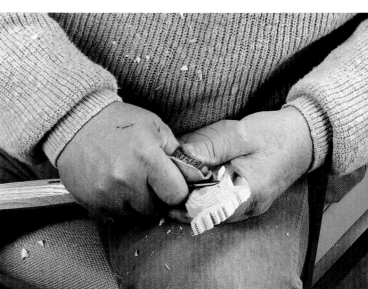

Use a gouge to cup out the wattle.

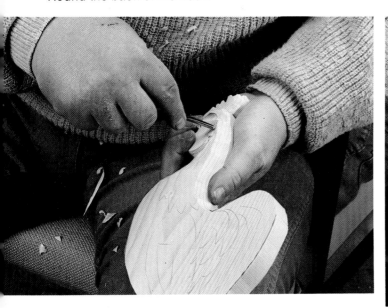

Cut stops at the back of the fluffy feathers that make up the ear.

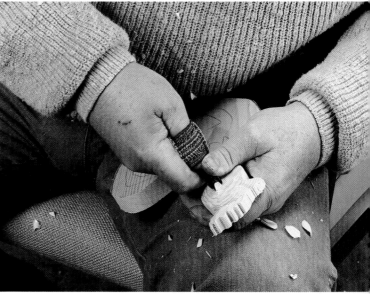

Gouge out the depression of the ear.

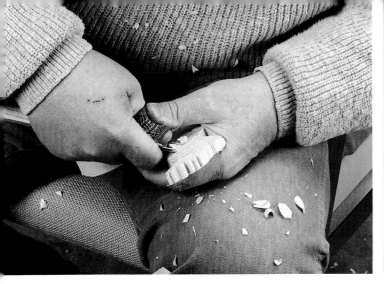

Use this thumb-lock position when carving in your lap. It gives you control of the chisel and keeps you from cutting yourself.

Round over the saddle using a gouge.

Put a stop in the jawline and...

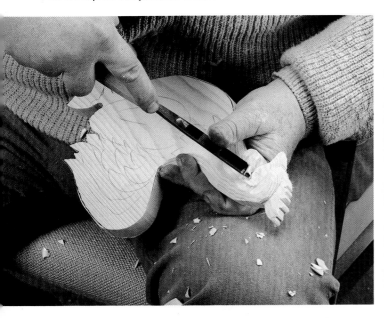

carve back up to it.

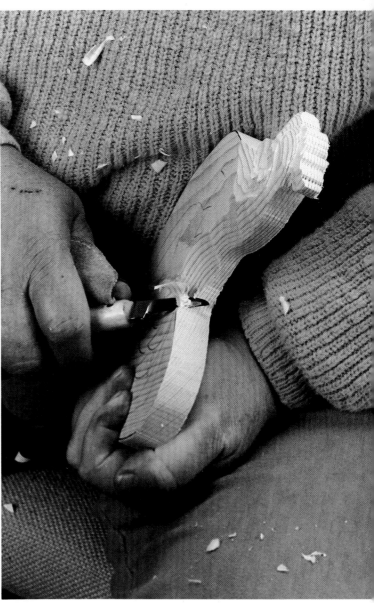

If that doesn't work, try a knife.

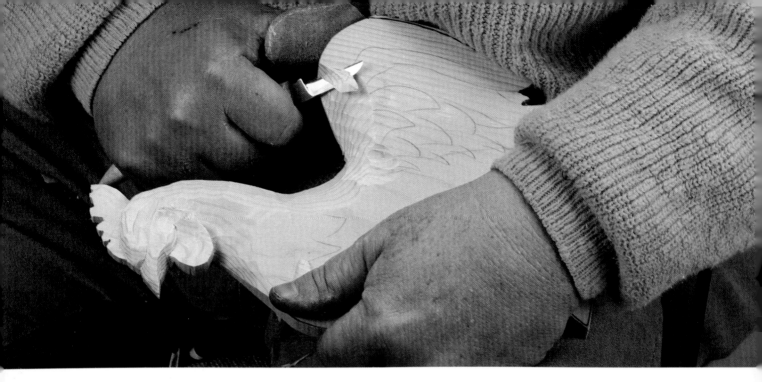

Continue the beveling around the tail.

Round off the breast.

The bold strokes give almost a feather effect, making our later finishing work easier.

Continue down to the feet.

Cut a stop around the front of the wing.

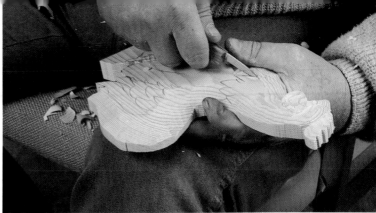

Cut back into the stop with a gouge from the breast. This also gives a feathery effect.

Cut a v-shaped notch into the bottom of the hackle...

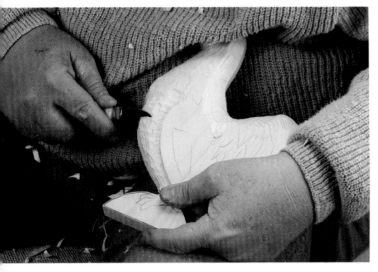

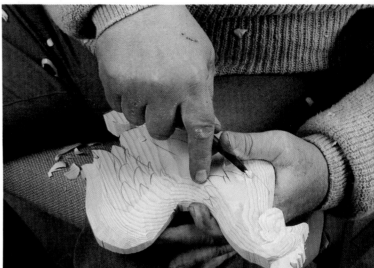

Trim down the breast with the knife.

and lift up the excess wood.

Redraw the neck hackle.

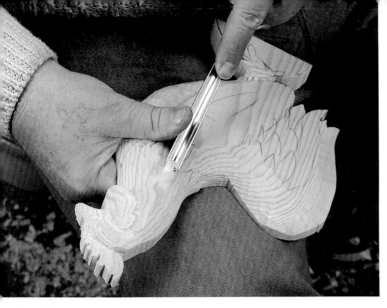 

Using your gouge, start at the bottom of the hackle and run long groves up the neck...

to the top of the head. These gouge marks will give the look of feathering.

The hackle will now look like this.

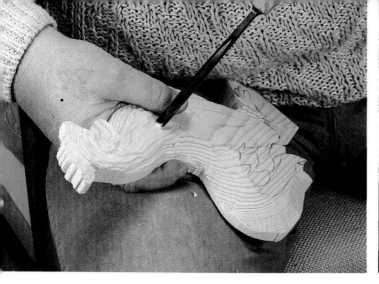

Cut some stops with a v-gouge to define shorter feathers in the hackle. You don't need too many of these.

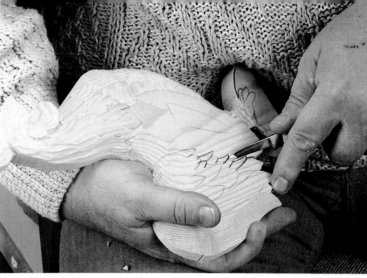

Use the knife to cut v-shaped stops at the bottom of the saddle hackle. Carve back to it from the body and remove the wood from the center of the "v".

Use the same tool to cut back to the stops from the bottom of the hackle.

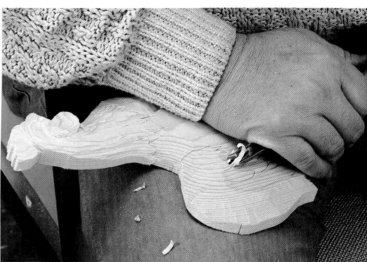

Use the gouge to cut grooves from the bottom of the saddle hackle upward in long strokes. Again this gives the look of feathers.

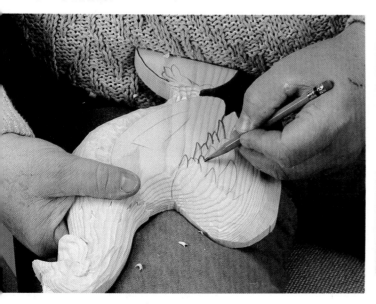

Remark the saddle hackle.

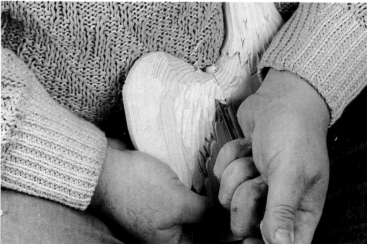

Using the large gouge like a palm gouge, add some smaller grooves, especially at the top of the saddle hackle.

Use the v-gouge to make stops and cut back to the stops to define other feathers in the hackle.

On the tail side of the line we made to define the saddle, use a flatter gouge to flatten the area and bring out and define the saddle area even more.

Use the v-gouge again to make a deep line between the saddle hackle and the ornamental feathers at the back of the rooster.

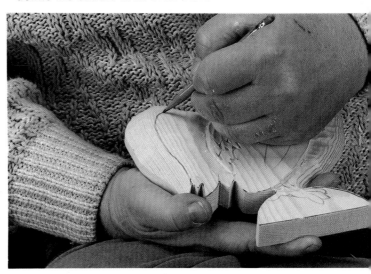

Since this is a barnyard rooster, only its ornamental tail feathers will show. In gamecocks, flight feathers also would be evident. Draw in the large outside ornamental feather first.

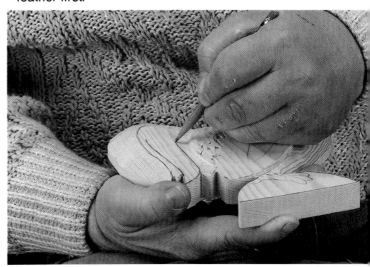

Then add the other long feathers.

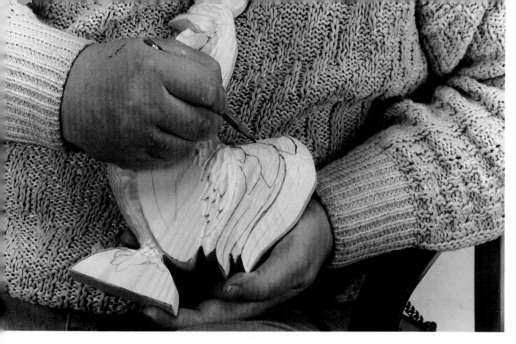

Finally, draw in the shorter, overlapping feathers.

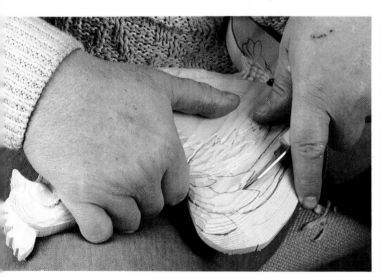

Cut out the v's where the feathers meet.

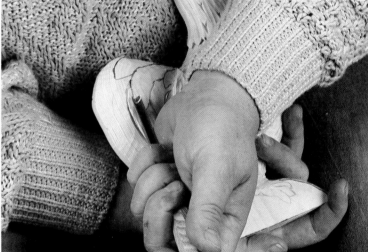

Start with the longer feathers and end with the shorter feathers.

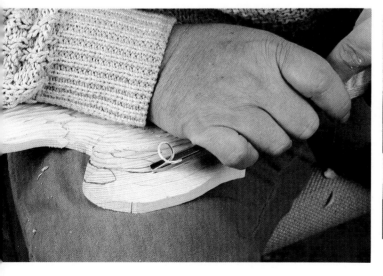

Cut the feather lines out with the v-gouge.

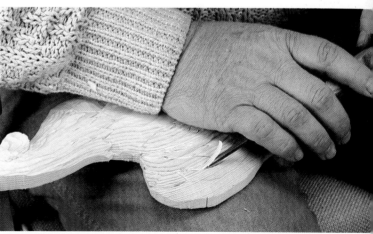

Using a flat chisel to create a deeper flat area between some of the feathers, give the tail area a three-dimensional look.

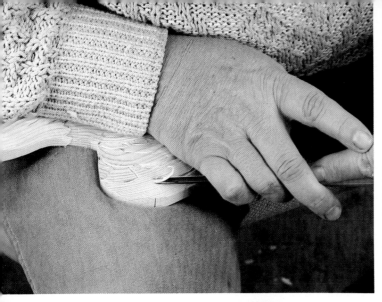

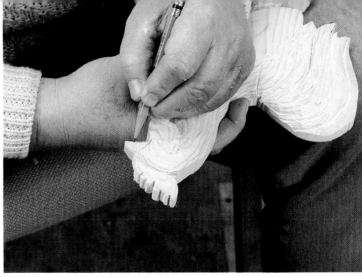

Draw in the beak...

Use a veiner to make grooves up the center of the feathers and define the quills.

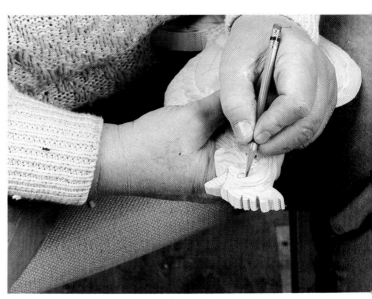

and the eye.

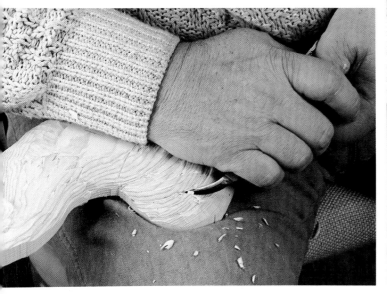

Clean up the lines in the tail area.

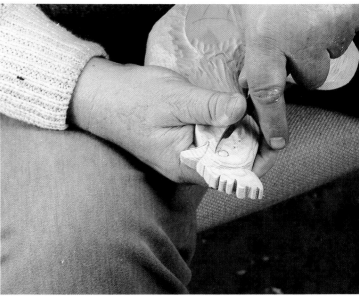

Start with a v-shaped notch in each corner of the eye...

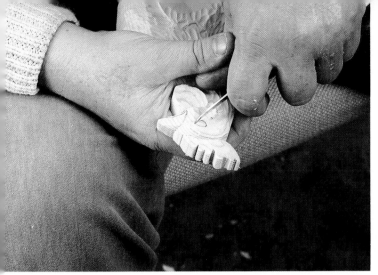

and at a flat angle, chip it out.

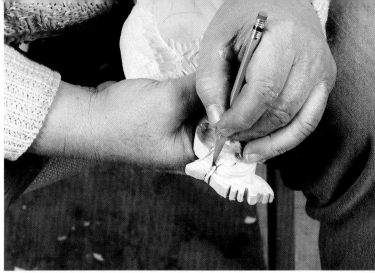

Prepare to carve the beak. I added the nose membrane at the top of the beak.

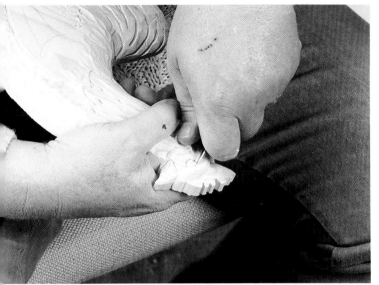

Cut a stop around the upper and lower eyelids...

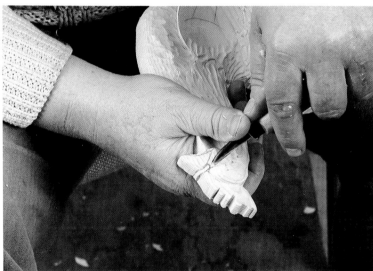

Starting at the corner, cut a stop and trim back to it.

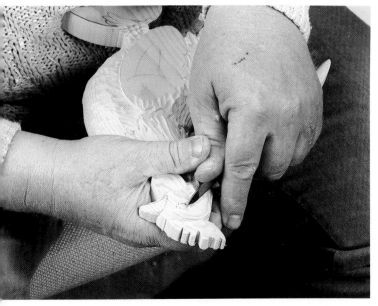

and round the eyeball over to it.

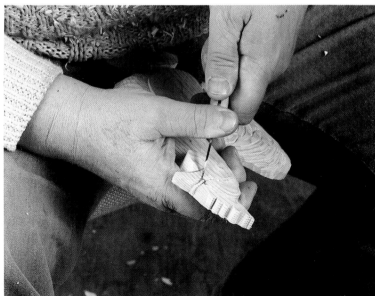

Continue around the back of the beak with a stop...

and a cut.

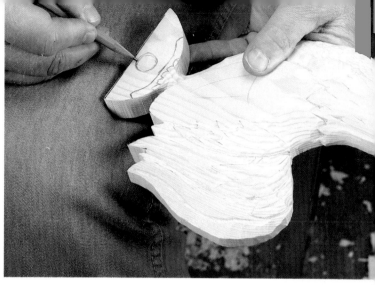

Mark the feet with feather tuft, foot, and a hole for a peg so we can use our rooster in the kitchen to hang pot holders.

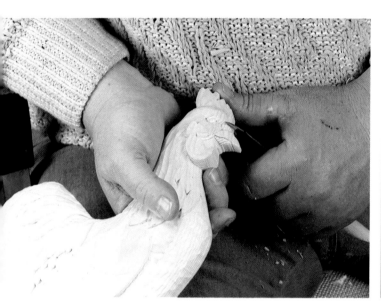

Trim back to the nose membrane.

Make a stop at the end of the talons...

Use a large nailset to make the pupil.

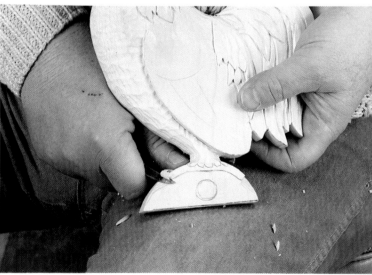

and trim back into it.

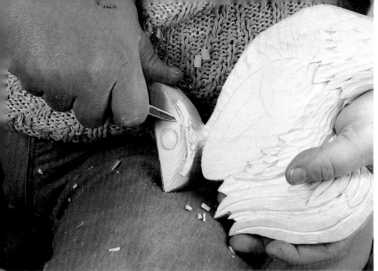

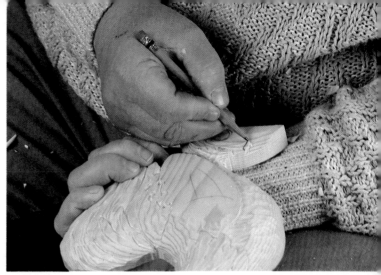

Carve a stop along the bottom of the foot and carve back into it, rounding the base.

Draw in the toenails, front and back...

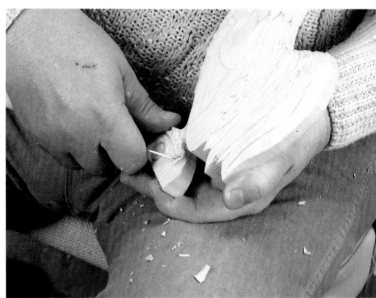

Do the same thing with the feathers, cutting a stop and cutting back to it from the feet. This also round off the top of the feet.

and cut them out.

Cut v-shaped stops in the bottom of feather tuft and pop out the excess wood to bring out the feather.

Remark the secondary flight feathers on the wings.

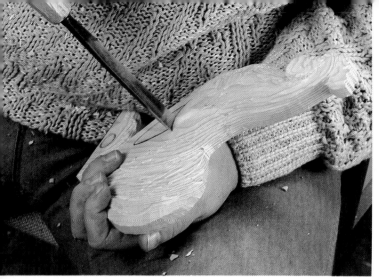

Use a gouge to cut stops on the line of the wing butt.

Cut back to it.

and use the gouge to trim back to it.

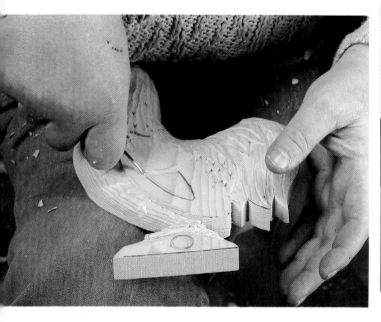

Cut a stop in the secondary feathers with a knife...

Take a gouge and go over everything, removing saw marks and simulating feathers.

This stroke will simulate the short feathers on the wing butt.

Drill a hole for a peg.

A nearly complete rooster.

Insert a commercially available shaker peg in the hole.
The rooster now may be used to hang potholders, towels,
or whatever.

Painting the Potholder Holder

For painting the flatcarvings we use a liquid acrylic paint. It comes in small plastic bottles and is available in a variety of colors at most craft stores and some fabric stores. It is often used for stenciling and other handicrafts. It gives the stronger color we want for this type of carving and dries quickly. The finish easily can be made to look antique.

Begin by painting the comb red. Use a plate as a palette and add a little water to the red to dilute it.

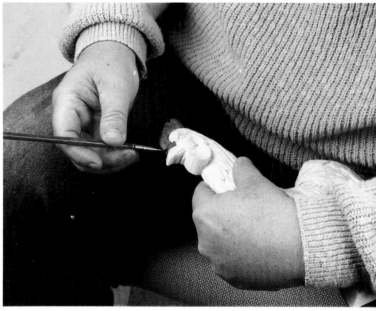

Continue down the bridge of the nose...

Apply the paint to the comb.

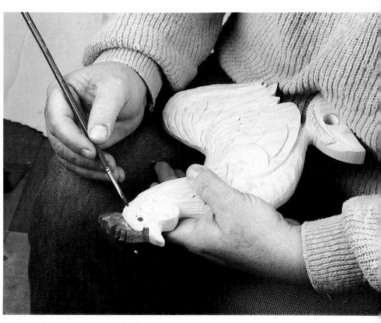

and the eye.

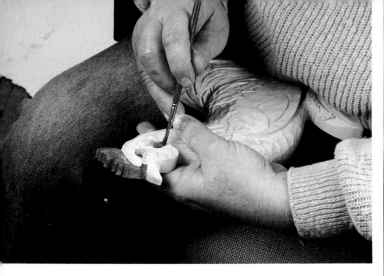

Apply a light red wash around the eye and on the ear wattles. These are points where the rooster's skin shows through the thinner layer of feathers.

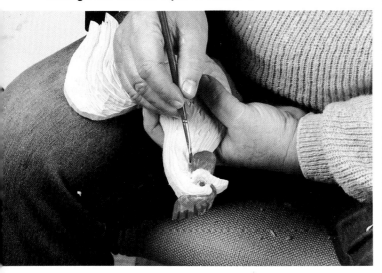

Return to the heavier red for the wattle under the chin.

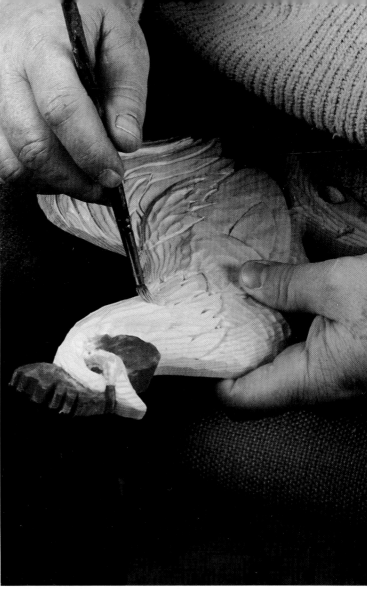

Use a larger brush to paint the breast and neck.

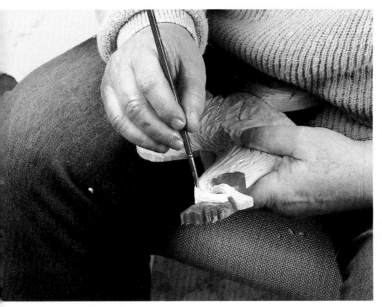

This barnyard chicken is black and white. Begin with white around the face and head.

Also paint the leg tufts white.

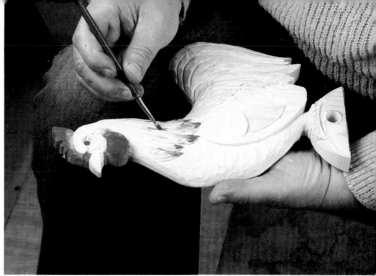

Make the end of the feathers darker red, continuing up the neck.

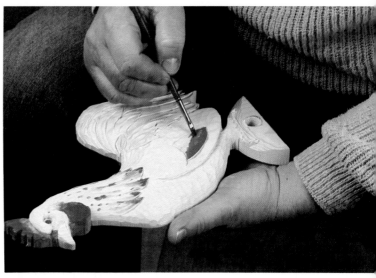

Paint the secondary flight feathers at the center of the wing red.

Paint the main part of the wing and the rest of the body white, leaving the center of the wing unpainted. Nothing is critical in painting the chicken, since a chicken could be almost any color in the rainbow.

Blend red streaks into the neck hackle, beginning at the bottom.

Paint the ornamental tail feathers black. Start at the bottom, using a large brush...

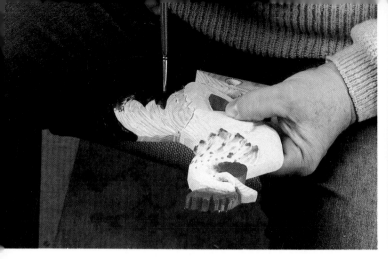

then get in the crooks and crannies using a smaller brush.

Add a few touches of this blending color to the breast...

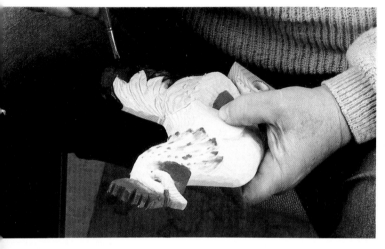

Blend a little red where the black meets the other feathers at the top. This will soften the harshness of the black meeting the white.

and the back.

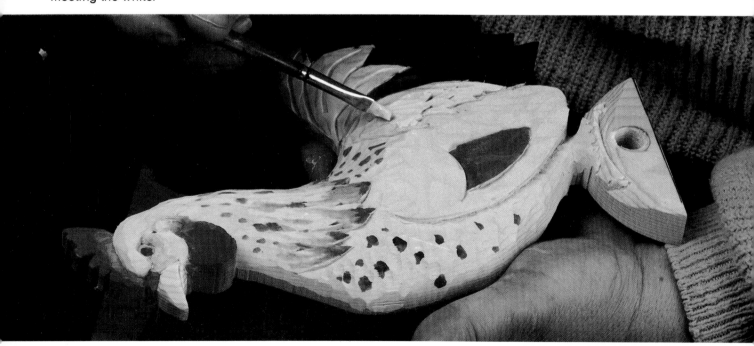

With a clean brush, give the tail hackles an undercoat.

Add red highlights to the tail hackles. This helps to balance the red in the head and neck area.

Paint the tips of the lesser ornamental feathers black.

The painting thus far.

Blend in red and carry the blended color to the top of the tails.

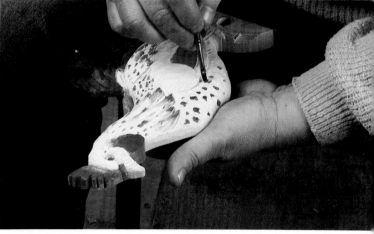

Add some red speckles to the breast and back.

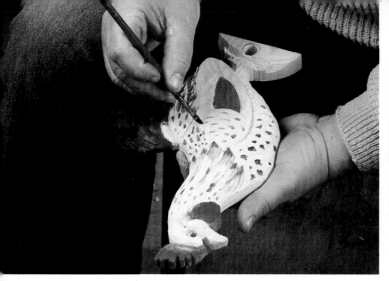

Cross strokes on the wings give the feeling of broader feathers.

Add a black speck to the eyeball.

Apply yellow to the beak...

and the feet.

The bird is complete except for the peg and ground area. These will be stained after the paint dries.

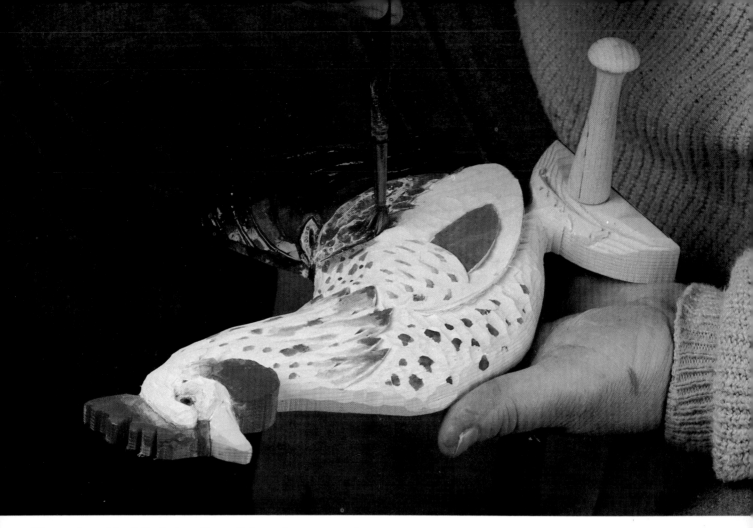

The antiqued look that gives these flat carvings some of their character comes from applying a varnish stain over the painted surface. They acquire instant aging. Apply the stain to the tail and back of the rooster with a brush.

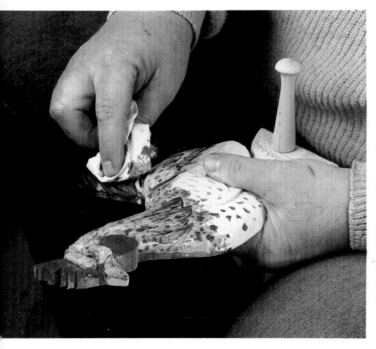

Wipe it off with a rag or paper towel.

Continue to apply stain to the rest of the rooster including the base and peg. Wipe this off too.

The complete rooster.

Carving a Welcome Sign

Make several copies of the pattern so you can cut them apart and lay a portion down for tracing on the wood.

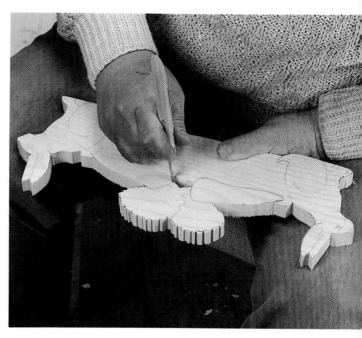

Drill the hole below the carrots and clean it up with a knife.

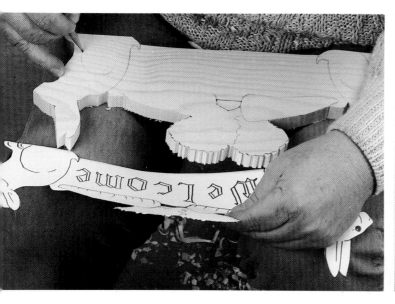

Use the pattern to mark the blank.

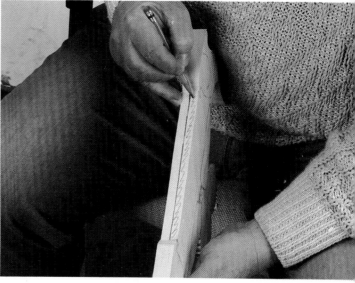

You want to lower the center area. I want to go about half the thickness of the board. This will define the base of the bas relief.

Cut stops around the drawings and cut back to them. Start with the corners. The cut will have be done over again and again until the board reaches the depth you desire.

Another view of edge work.

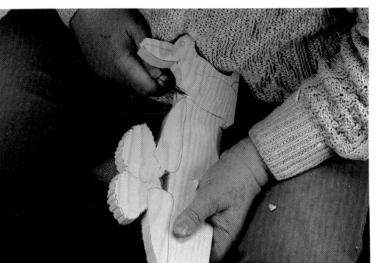

Trim around the figures and the bottom edge first.

The finished groove around the edge.

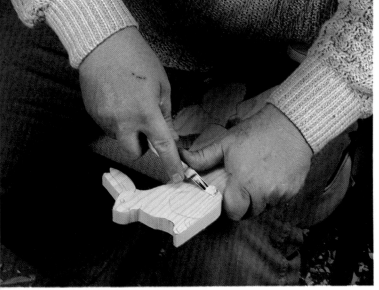

For some of this edge work, a gouge works nicely.

Remove the wood from the sign area with a gouge across the grain.

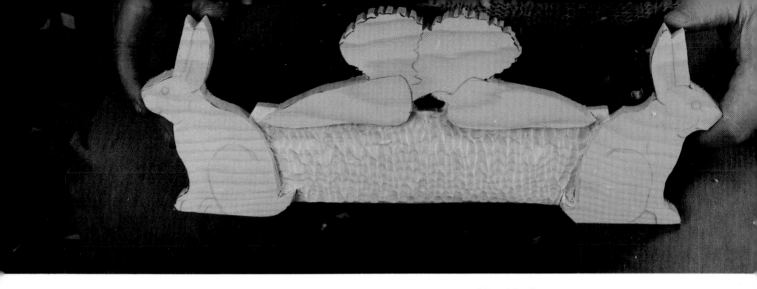

After the first gouging, the piece will have a ridged look like this.

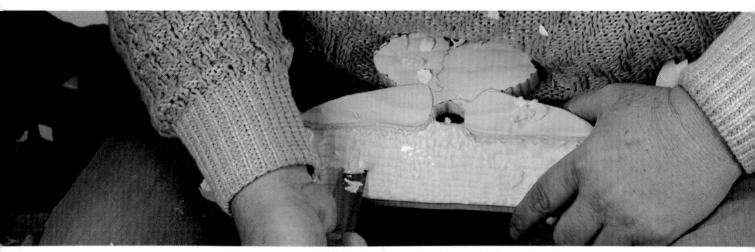

Now take a flatter, wider gouge and smooth the sign area.

The sign area is prepared.

Go around the silhouette of the carrots with a perimeter stop. Make the edge ragged around the carrot top.

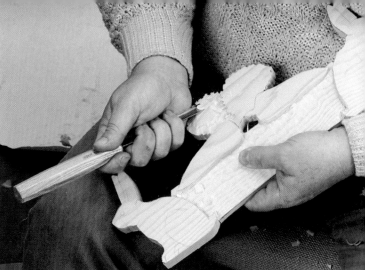

Gouge the top of the back/lower carrot using short cuts. This gives the carrot greens effect.

Carve away the stem so it is lower and appears to go into the center of the carrot top.

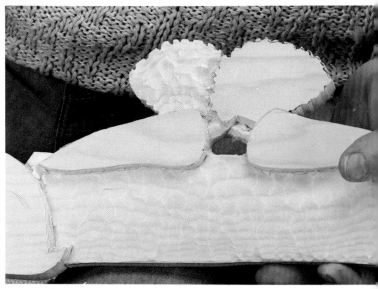

Cut into the stop with a gouge from the lower carrot.

The two stems cross, so one needs to look like it is going over the other.

Do the upper carrot top in the same way. Start by cutting into the stop...

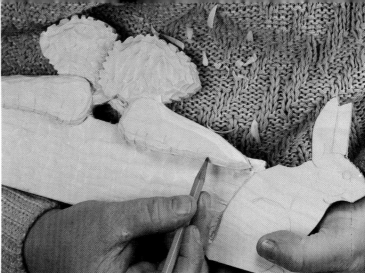

Draw in the marks on the carrots...

then gouge the surface with short strokes.

and cut lightly with a veiner.

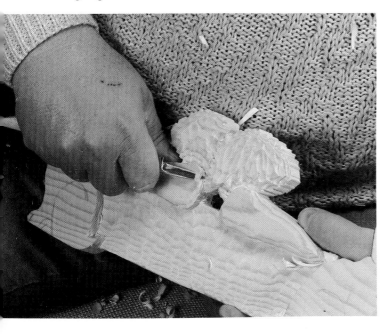

Round the edges of the carrots.

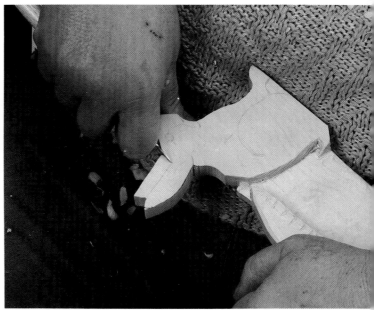

Cut a stop on the lines between the two ears.

Cut back to the stop, going with the grain and using a knife.

The trimmed ear.

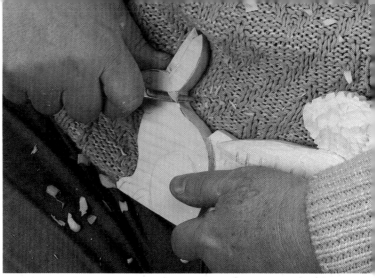

Cut a notch at the bottom of the ears so they seem to come into the side of the head instead of the top.

Thin the neck and give it shape from front to back.

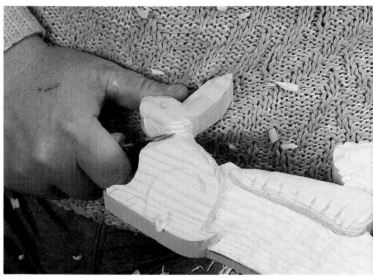

This defines the shoulder and jawline. The jaw should be square at this point. The shoulder should be rounded.

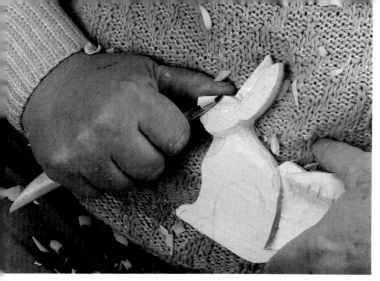

Go around the cheek, trimming and defining the muzzle.

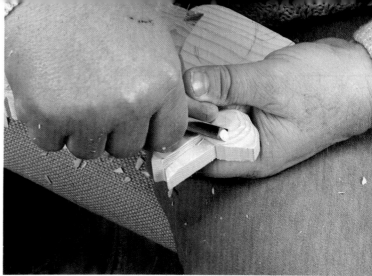

Cut an eye socket with a palm gouge.

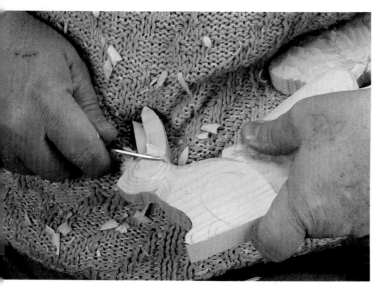

Continue to round under the chin and at the base of the ears.

Round the back of the rabbit.

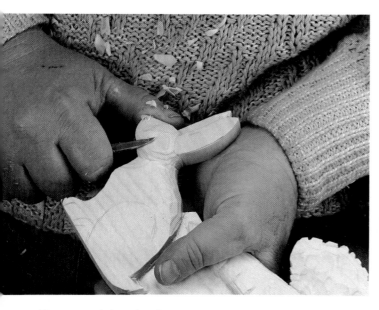

Now round the cheek.

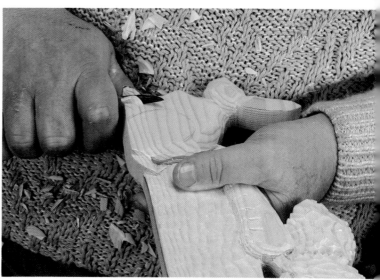

After you've finished rounding the back, define the back paw by thinning the front paw.

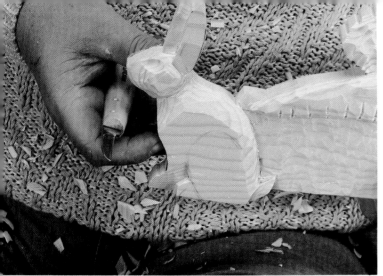

It should look something like this.

Gouge around the outside of the haunch line.

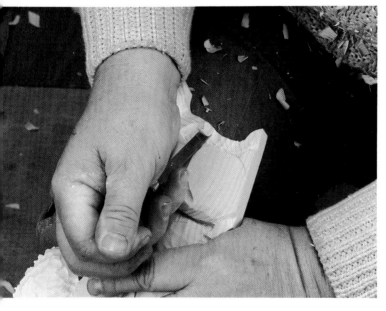

Round the breast and the front leg with a palm gouge.

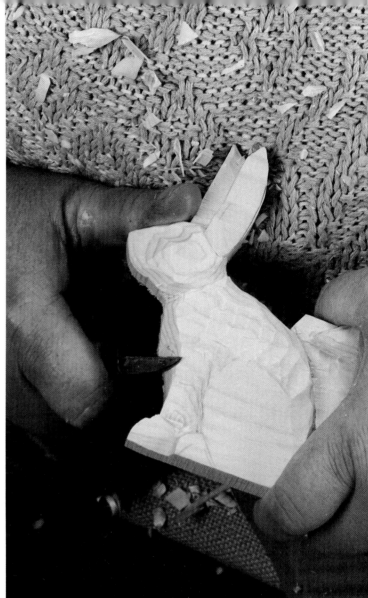

Bring out the front line of the front leg with the knife.

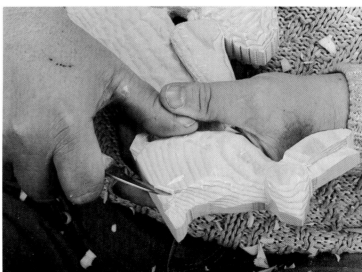

Trim down the back foot by cutting a stop on its line with the haunch and cutting back to it. The foot should be rounded, not flat.

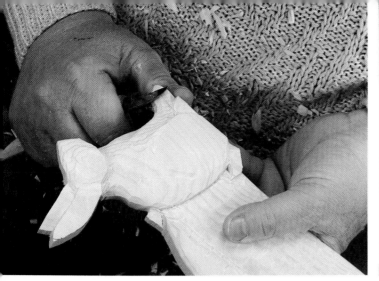

Trim and round the front feet.

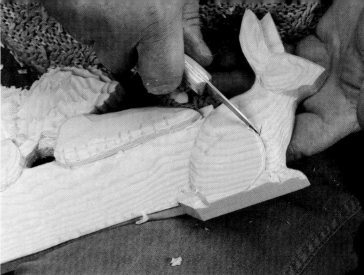

Cut a v where the legs meet...

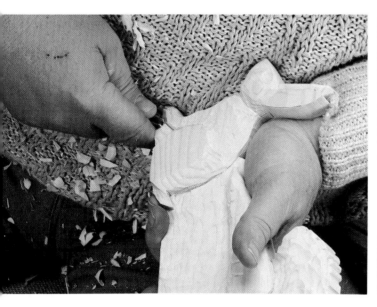

Cut the toes with the v-shaped gouge.

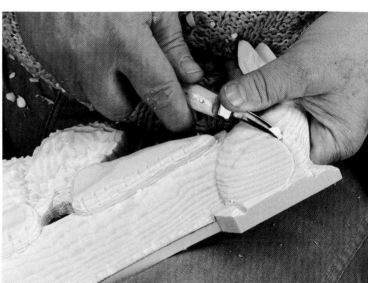

and pop out the wood.

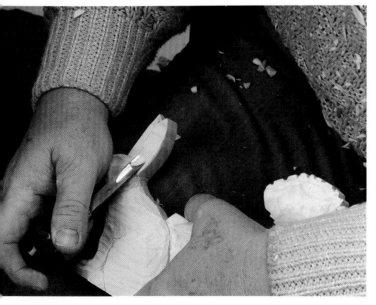

Clean the inside of the ears with a palm gouge.

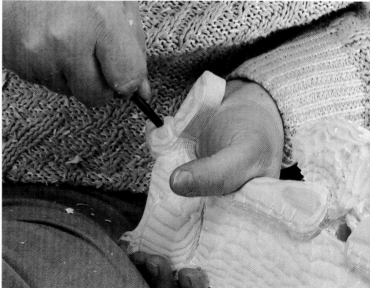

Mark the iris with a large nailset.

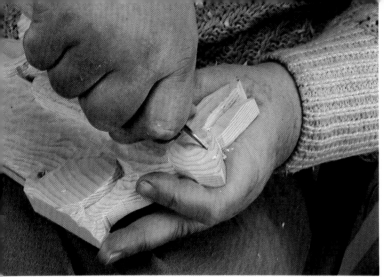

Cut a "v" in the corners of the eyes...

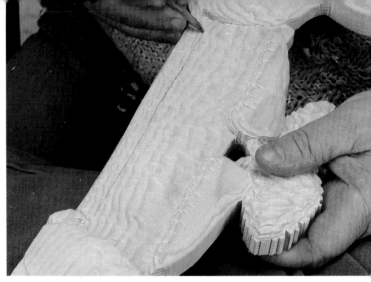

Make a line parallel to the bottom of the board, using your finger as a guide.

and cut back to them with a flat cut to get the shape of the eyeball.

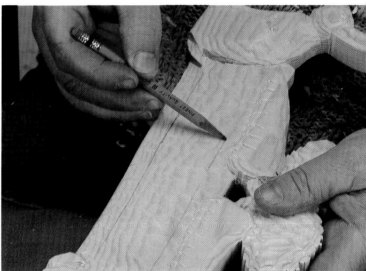

Another line marks the height of tall letters.

A finished rabbit.

Mark the center with a vertical line...

and make one more horizontal line to indicate the height of the lowercase letters.

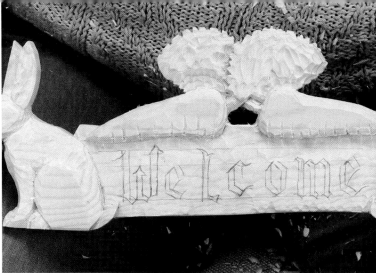

The letters drawn in place.

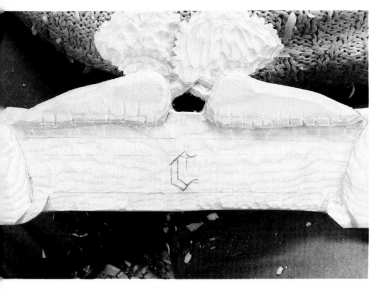

"Welcome" has seven letters with "c" in the center. Make your "c" so it lines up with your center mark.

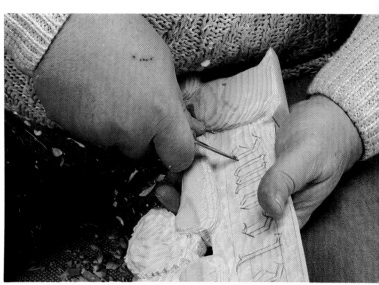

Incise cuts straight into the wood to put the stops at the end of lines of the letters.

Work your way out from the "c" on either side. This will help keep everything in balance.

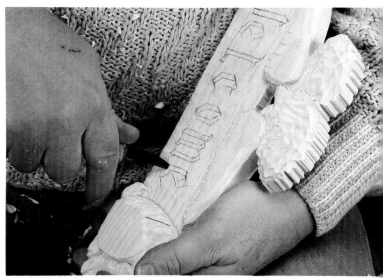

Use the knife to follow the letter's lines, cutting at a forty-five-degree angle.

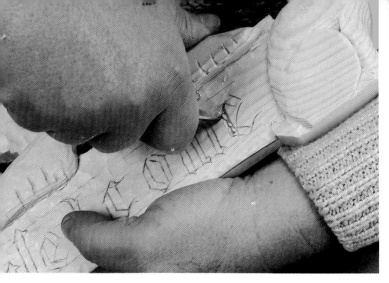

Carve back on the other side. Keep doing this until it falls out without popping it out. Do it over until it is clear. Do one part of the letter at a time.

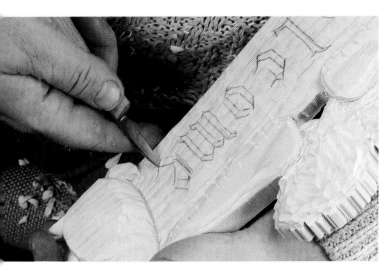

First cut the stop.

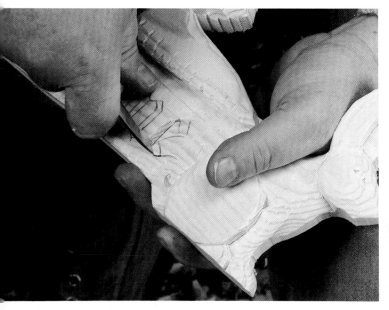

Then cut the forty-five-degree angle.

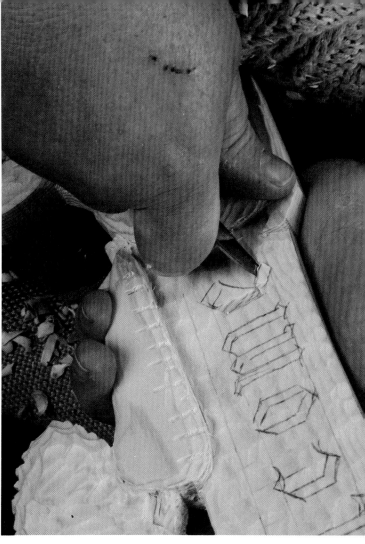

And finally cut a forty-five-degree angle on the other side until the middle comes out.

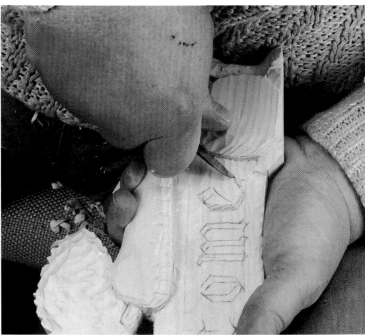

On the thin line, simply cut out a thin wedge.

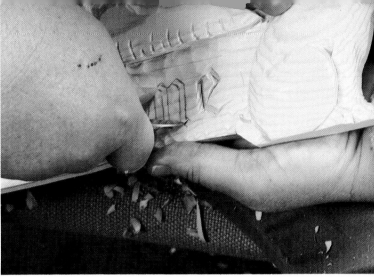

When the letter is done, go back and clean.

then the other.

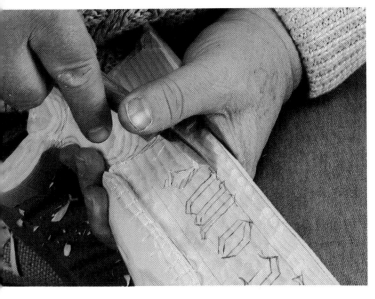

On letters like the "m," the end comes to a little diamond-shaped knob. Instead of a straight stop, you need to use a v-shaped stop on these letters. First cut on one side of the bottom...

Use a wide chisel to erase the guidelines you drew earlier. Do it lightly.

The carved welcome sign.

Painting a Welcome Sign

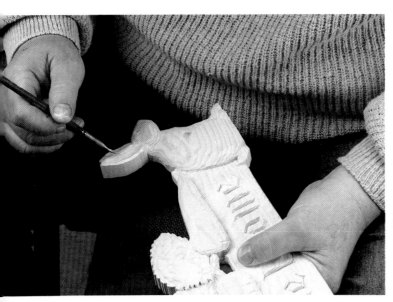

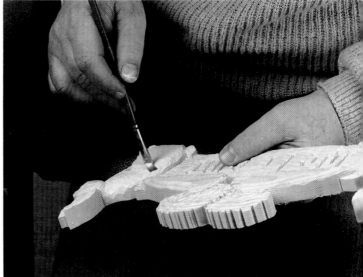

Paint the rabbits white all over.

The finished rabbits.

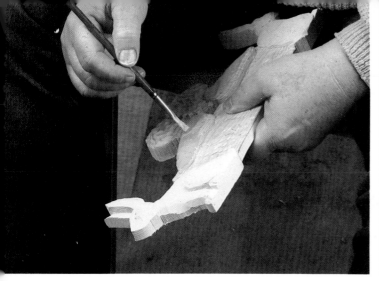

Paint the carrots orange.

The finished carrots.

Blend in a little pure yellow for a highlight on the top edge.

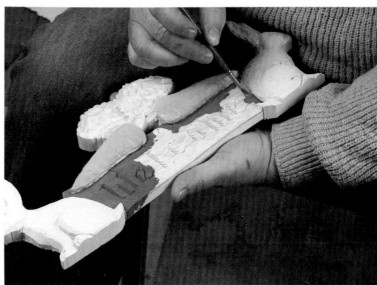

Paint the sign area blue, using a smaller brush for the edges...

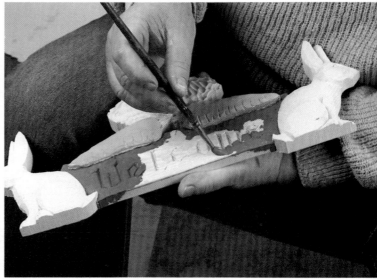

and a broader brush for the main area.

The finished sign.

Use a light green around the top of the carrot tops.

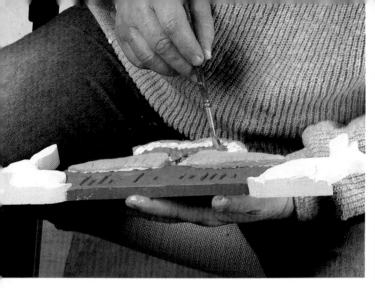

Paint a darker green around the bottom and stems.

The sign so far.

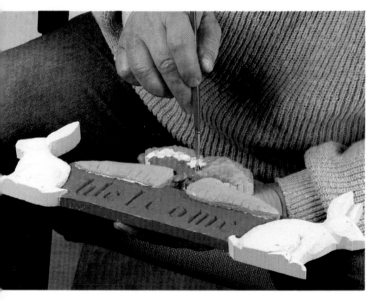

Splotch around between the two of them, using a medium green and blending as you go. You want a splotchy look.

Add red to the rabbit's eyes.

Blend the greens together.

Paint the inside of the rabbit's ears pink.

The painting is complete.

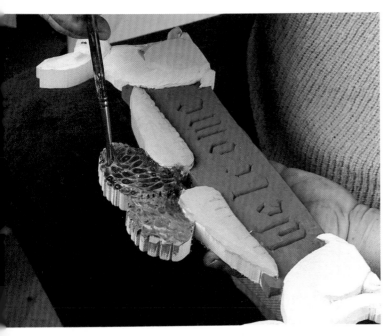

Like the other pieces, the antique effect is obtained by adding stain over the sign and wiping it off. Begin with the carrots.

Then do the face of the sign. Put an ample amount in the letters.

Finally stain the rabbits and wipe them off almost immediately. You don't want the stain to set too long on the white. Continue wiping off the whole sign.

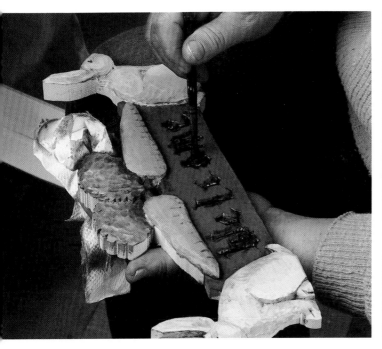

Reapply stain in the letters.

Wipe the sign down one final time and let it dry.

Carving the Man In The Moon

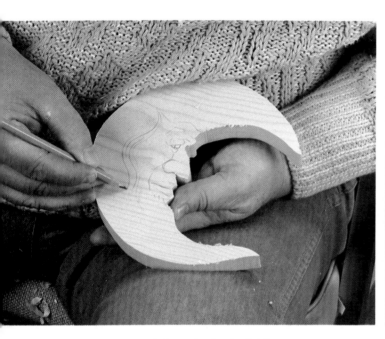

Cut the pattern and draw in the facial features.

and continue down the nose.

Gouge the eye with a palm gouge...

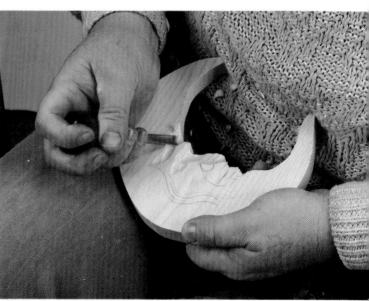

Also use the gouge to cut down the forehead. This will leave the eyebrows protruding.

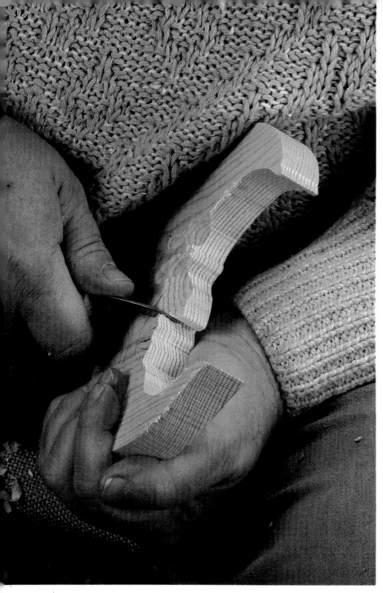

Use a gouge to go around the nostril flare.

Cut a good strong stop at the bottom of the nose...

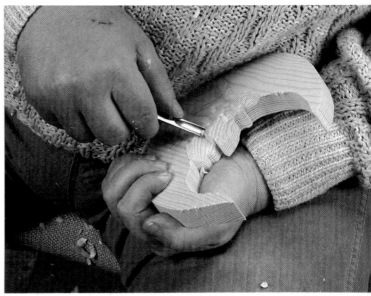

Trim back to it from the cheek.

and trim up to it from the lip. Be careful not to cut the nose.

Define the top of the nostril with a gouge.

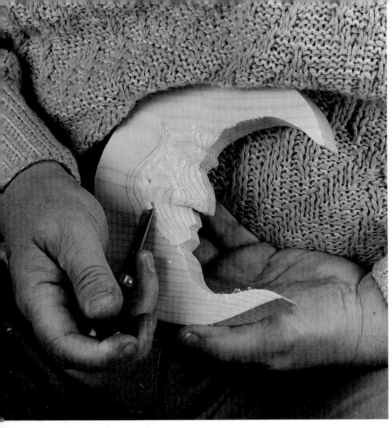

Follow the hairline with the palm gouge.

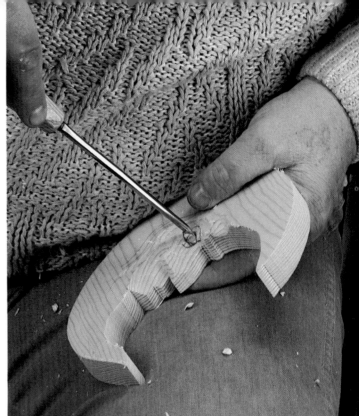

Using a gouge, cut a stop around the eyelid.

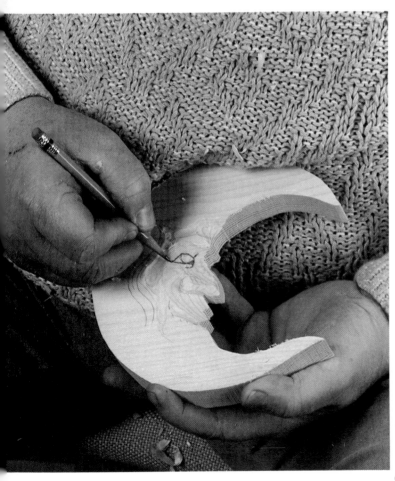

Draw in the lines of the eye.

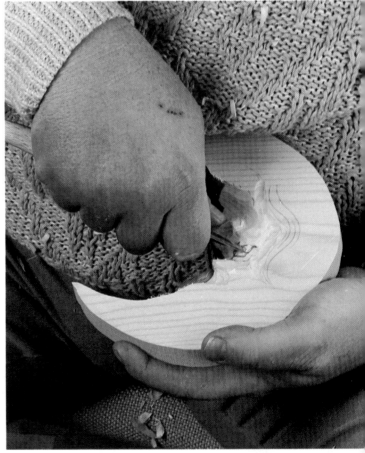

Cut out the back corner at a flat angle to give shape to the eyeball.

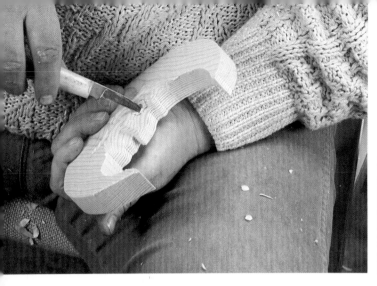

Do the same thing in the front corner.

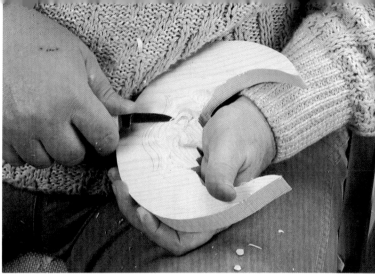

Put a little crow's foot in the corner of the eye.

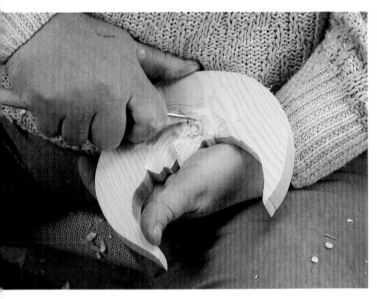

Cut a notch around the top of the lid to make it more prominent.

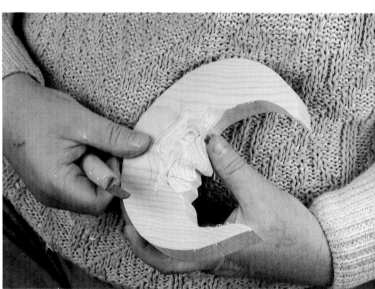

Draw in the mouth.

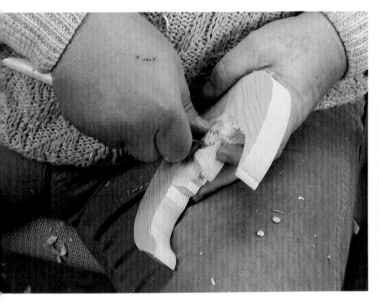

Do the same thing to the bottom lid.

Carve the lips in toward where they meet.

Cut the cheek line with a v-shaped cut.

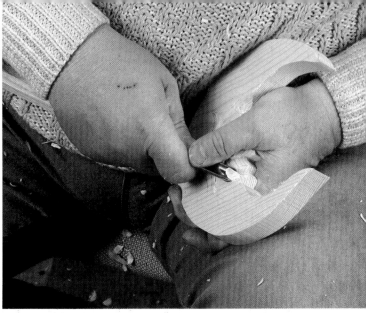

Gouge the area under the bottom lip.

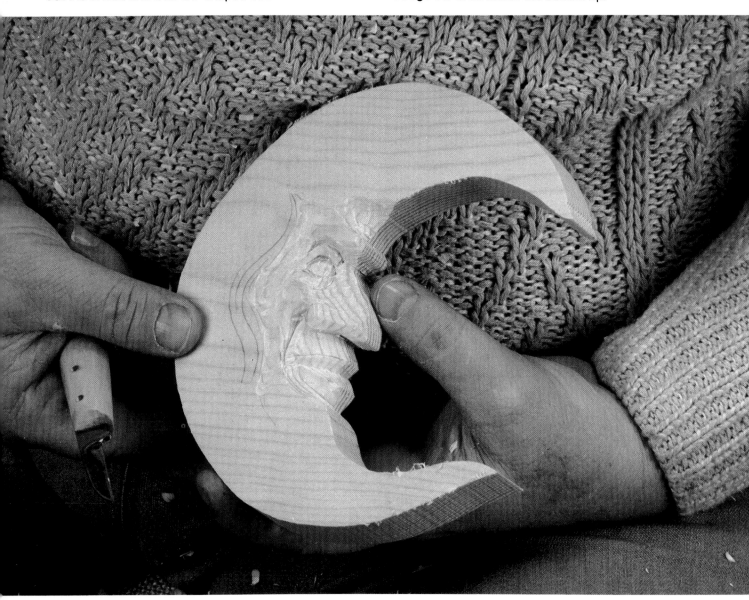

Add character lines around the mouth.

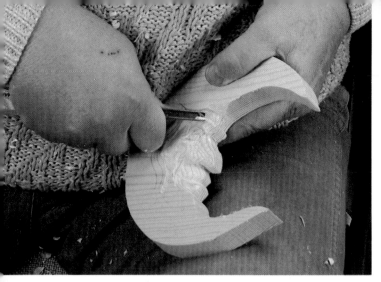

Put hair strokes in the eyebrows with a v-gouge.

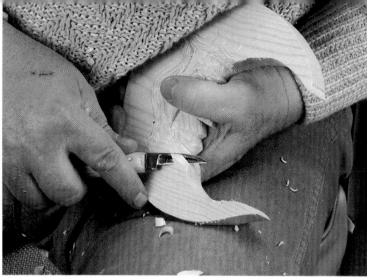

Round the chin off...

Continue adding hair with the v-gouge to the top of the head...

and continue putting hair on the beard.

and the side.

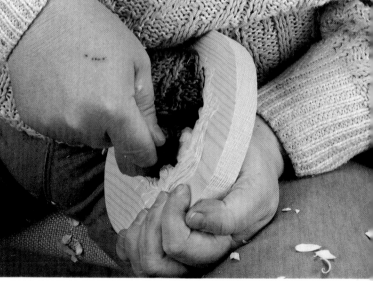

Make the eyeball with the large nailset.

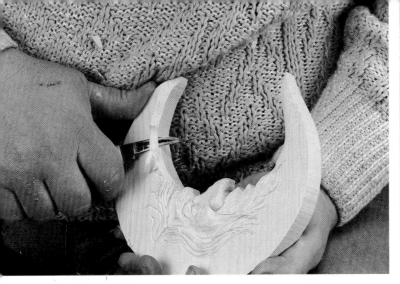

Taper the ends of the crescent and bevel the inside edge slightly.

Go over the moon lightly with the knife

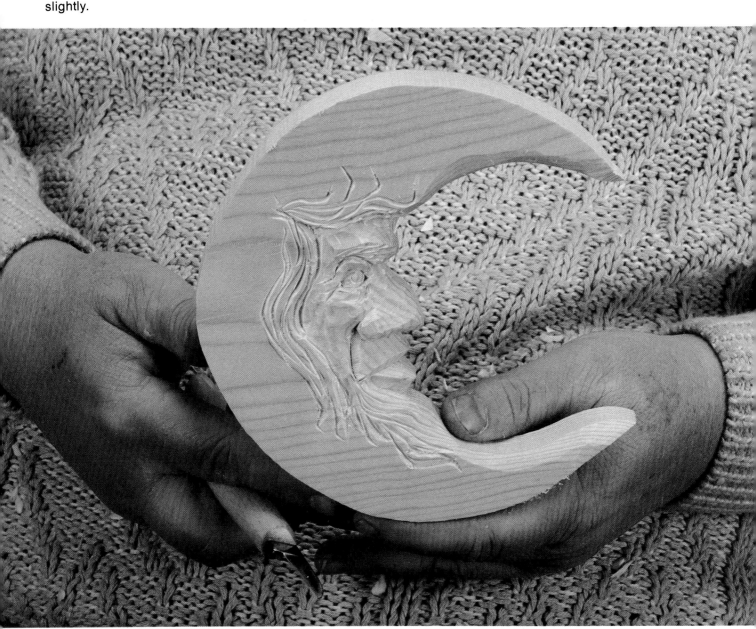

The finished carving.

Painting the Man In The Moon

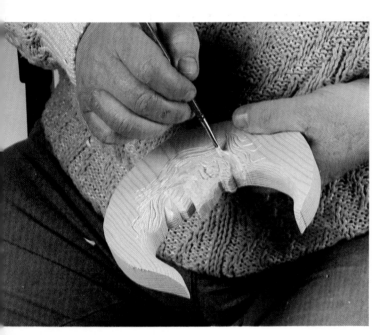

Apply flesh color to the face.

Use a plate or aluminum pie tin to blend the paints.

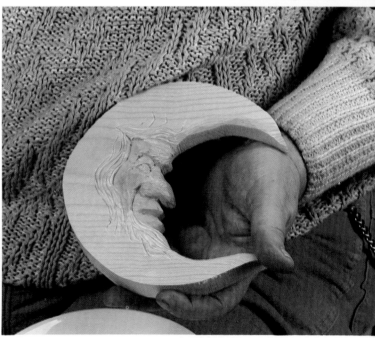

Apply a redder color to the cheeks, nose, and lips. Spread, blend, and lighten if necessary.

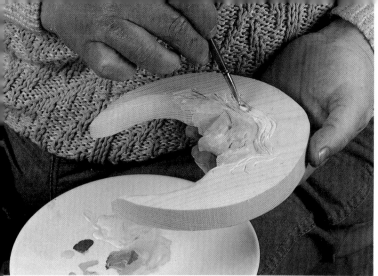

Apply an off-white color to the hair areas around the face.

Now to make our moon blue. Use enough water with the blue paint to form a wash.

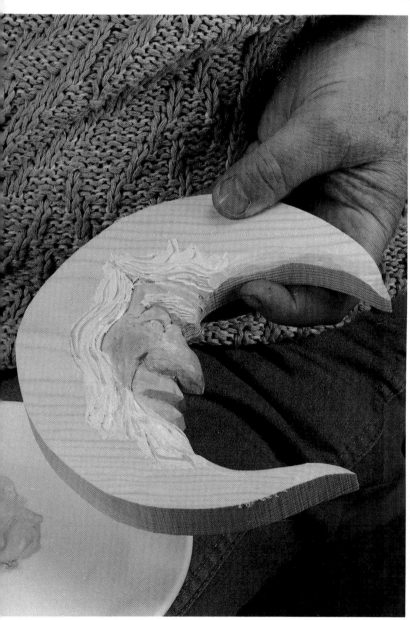

Blend the blue into the white.

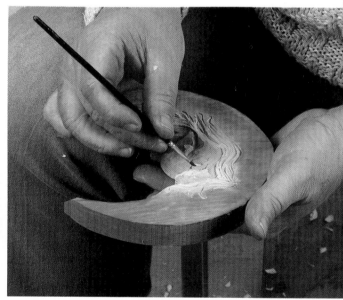

The face with the white applied.

Paint the eye with white.

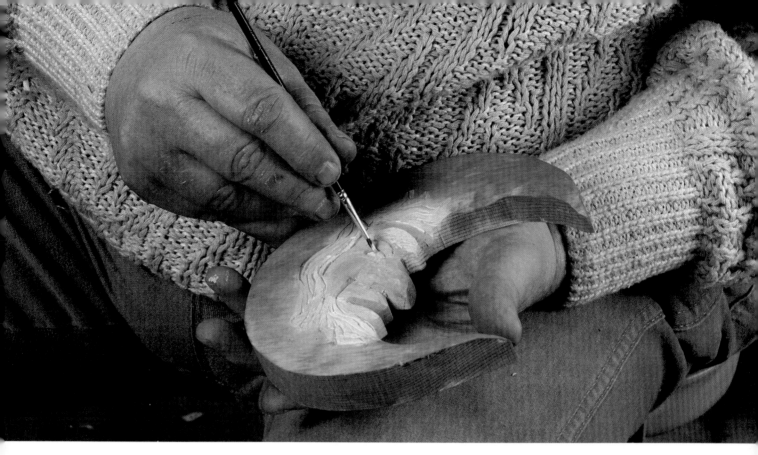

Add blue to the iris.

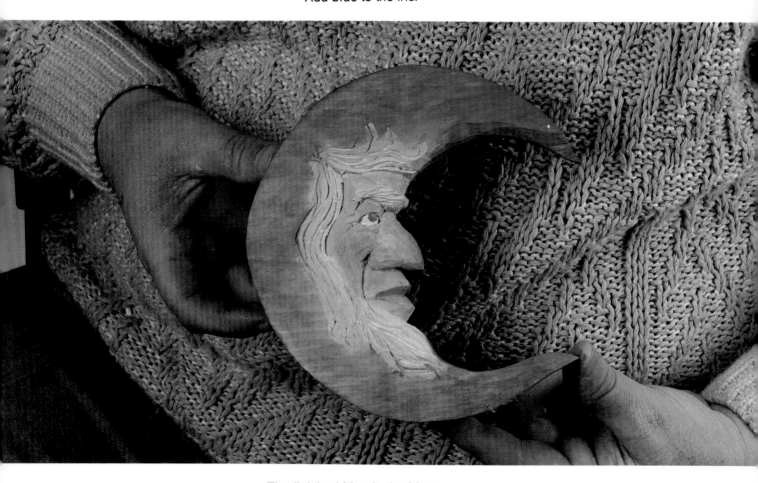

The finished Man in the Moon.

Apply stain to the whole carving.

Wipe off the excess.

Finished!